Equally Yoked; The Four Keys to a Successful Marriage in God's Kingdom

Equally Yoked; The Four Keys to a Successful Marriage in God's Kingdom

Equally Yoked; The Four Keys to a Successful Marriage in God's Kingdom

EQUALLY YOKED

THE FOUR KEYS TO A SUCCESSFUL MARRIAGE IN GOD'S KINGDOM

By
Ervin Koe Jones III

Equally Yoked
The Four Keys to a Successful Marriage in God's Kingdom

By Ervin Koe Jones III

Copyright © 2021

Printed in the United States of America
Catalogued in the Library of Congress

ISBN: 13: 978-1735333014

<u>Published by</u>
True Faith Consulting & Publishing

Unless otherwise noted, all Scripture quotations are taken from the King James and the New International Version of the Bible.

All Rights Reserved. No part of this book may be reproduced or transmitted in any form or by any means, electronically or mechanically, including photocopying recording, and/or by any other information storage and retrieval system, without written permission in writing from the publisher.

DEDICATION

This book is dedicated to "EM" my first wife. She was a great encouragement in my life. Thank you for helping me find my way to manhood.

EM, for years I wanted to tell you that we could have worked things out if I had only put God first in our relationship. So, I pray that God bless and cover you in all things that you do, as well as give you a man who loves you like Christ loves the church.

I also, dedicate this book to singles who want to do it God's way because his way will work. And, to those who are married, I likewise pray this book will encourage and remind you why you got married and that you remember the true reason for marriage is to glorify God.

TABLE OF CONTENTS

INTRODUCTION………………………………...13

PRAYER......……………………………………19

PART ONE………………………………….21

Be Equally Yoked in Christ

PART TWO…………………………………33

Counting the Cost in the Relationship

PART THREE……………………………...39

Denying Yourself

Pick up Your Cross and Follow Me

PART FOUR………………………………..49

Renewing Your Mind

CONCLUSION………………………………..57

INTRODUCTION

The first key to note is that marriage is in fact to glorify God, and by doing that effectively, you would express affection for others and know that it can work and be successful. We must be willing to sacrifice and stay steadfast in His Word so that God will get all the praise and glory, and by extension, others too, will get saved through our relationship because they would want to know the God that we serve. One of the most critical factors about walking this life is that it is not about you or your personal feelings or things going your way, but it is allowing the Heavenly Father to have His way in all of your life.

I will break down the four keys while I discuss the relationships that I have been in and why they did not work and the reason it will work now. This knowledge can be particularly challenging for most people because they choose not to believe, but scriptures will be used throughout this book from

God's word to help support the claim. My personal experience and the scriptures do line up, and I know that you can have a true successful marriage in the Kingdom of God. I will first look at our personal relationship with Christ, which means that we are to be equally yoked, individually, and together as a couple. This means that we both need to be saved, worshipping the same God, and be willing to give our lives to Him.

Many times, most individuals get married for all the wrong reasons, such as financial needs or they may feel it is just the right thing to do. They do not utterly understand the consequences involved. Suppose you are not equally yoked or on the same page spiritually? In that case, the marriage will not work no matter what you do because having a solid foundation in Christ is essential to any relationship. You would need to be in a relationship with Christ before being in a relationship with another person. Therefore, your marriage should start with your relationship with God, to allow God to work within your union with another person. That would be the first key to having a relationship with Christ, being equally yoked in Christ and with one another.

The second key is counting the spiritual cost of the relationship. Many people fail to count the cost because they do not understand that there is a cost associated in getting married or what it means to count the cost in the relationship. The real reason for getting married should be to spend the rest of your life with this individual – for better or worse. By God's way, there will be no way out, no divorce decree, purely biblical commitment, and rightly so, because you would have done what He required of you before you take the next step.

The third key looks at denying yourself and picking up the cross. Unfortunately, many people do not know the extent of denying themselves and truly picking up their cross so they can walk the pathway that God walks. But I intend to break it down with scriptures. As I discussed earlier in the chapter, our marriage and living the life we were created for means doing it all for God. Denying yourself is not about an individual or their personal opinion but giving God all the praise, glory, and honor due unto Him in their marriage.

The fourth key is to renew the mind by being still. This is one of the most challenging of all the four points because it entails sitting down, being still, and giving it all to God daily, recognizing that He alone has the answer to all the situations that people face. Psalm 46:10 says, "Be still and know that I am God. I will be exalted among the heathen; I will be exalted among the earth." It allows you to realize that you can do nothing without Christ being the foundation of your life, and He is the one who strengthens you. By renewing my mind, it lets me know that I am not in control of my life and that it is all about God. I am learning that I must ride in the car's trunk and not tell God to take the wheel and then try to take the wheel myself. Riding in the car's trunk makes me live by faith and trusting God with my relationship, knowing that I need help in this relationship. I will renew my mind and tell my wife, "honey, I will lead by example and not tell you to do something that I would not do first." Those are a brief synopsis of the four keys of a successful marriage that must be utilized for success to be present in the union.

Several persons have indicated different keys to a successful marriage, but these are biblical from God's perspectives and what it should look like in God's Kingdom. Marriages can be victorious, it can be prosperous, and we can live a powerful life so that God's name alone be glorified.

The Four Keys

- ❖ **The first key** to note is that marriage is in fact to glorify God.
- ❖ **The second key** is counting the spiritual cost of the relationship.
- ❖ **The third key** looks at denying yourself and picking up the cross.
- ❖ **The fourth key** is to renew the mind by being still.

PRAYER

My Prayers go out to the people who want to do it God's way. I pray that these four keys help people in their marriage because we are not alone in this walk. Lord, also, please help young singles apply these four keys as they go through marriage counseling in-order to be open to one another. Lord, I also pray that this book be for your glory and people can grow doing things your way.

Part 1
Be Equally Yoked In Christ

The first key to a successful marriage is to glorify God; a personal relationship that is rooted in Christ. We need to focus on a relationship with God before we try to develop a relationship with others. Many people may miss out on this crucial point, especially if they are not always in His Word. In Matthew 6:33, it says, seek the Kingdom of God above all else, and live righteously, and he will give you everything you need (NLT). Rightly so, because having a relationship with Jesus Christ and God can benefit you in your interactions with another human being. I am a firm believer that if you have a vertical line, you can also have a horizontal line. What I mean by that is; personally, I did not understand what genuine relationships were about because most of my contacts were based on physical attraction.

I did not understand what a Christlike marriage should be like or what dating an individual should feel like because I was not accustomed to seeing good marriages or having wonderful dating experiences because I was walking with my eyes closed. After all, marriage was predestined by God. I dated because others were doing it, but I was never into dating because I was more focus on being an athlete, a hustler, and selling drugs on the streets. The thing is, I did not understand the seriousness of marriage.

We need to focus on a relationship with God before we try to develop a relationship with others

When going through marriage, I learned that I had to find my way back to Christ. I gave my life to Christ when I was 19 years old, but I did not have a relationship with Him until I was 40 years old, so I was lost and had to rekindle my relationship with Him. My early experience growing up was dating many different types of girls in college, and outside the college, so it was all about sexual encounters, and not getting to know them individually. It was not about how to become one with them, emotionally or spiritually, it was all about getting sexually satisfied, but I did not know there was more to this life than pure sex. I did not know that God wanted me to have a better relationship and to be married. I did not think it was His plan for my life; instead, I was out there being a "male-ho" and a gigolo. I never thought about getting married or having the right foundation within my life, because you cannot want something that you do not know exist.

The best relationship that I had while in college was when I dated a girl named Nora. I felt that I genuinely loved and cared about her, and my foster mother, who was my best friend and died in a car accident, liked her. This relationship was different, and I felt she would be my wife one day, but then shortly after my mother passed, I learned that she was pregnant and had aborted our child. I was devastated, and it "ripped" a hole in my heart. I did not know the proper way to vent, express myself, or even communicate with her and, therefore, chose to turn my back on her and the relationship, and that hurt her. When I lost my foster mother, I also lost her, I closed my heart, and since then, I have never been the same person again. I ended up losing everything that meant something to me because I did things my way and not God's way.

I never thought about the relationship again. This girl was different, she was the first person I felt I ever loved, and I believed she was the best person for me. When I looked into her eyes, I knew that she loved me, but I did not try to make it work. I allowed her to leave and go with everything, including my athletic ring and my jacket. I dropped her like a "bad habit." I could not cope with my foster mother's death,

I knew she was the one

or the abortion (my girlfriend allowed her mother to have her do). I cannot say if it were a blessing or a curse, but the thing I know is that I was badly hurt, and I chose to hurt her to quench my own anger. And to this day, I pray that she will forgive me because I did not know how to vent or deal with this type of situation and explain to her how I was feeling.

I WAS 20 YEARS OLD AND TRYING TO FIND GOD

I went to different churches, tried different avenues and routes, but nothing actually gave me the fulfillment I felt I needed. Instead, I was following the practices of men and not realizing that I needed to have a personal relationship with Christ, which would in fact help me have a personal relationship with people. It was one of the hardest things for me as a young man growing up, learning for the first time that my relationship with Christ was predominantly the most important thing for it is the primary key to any connection or involvement in God's kingdom. First, knowing that we are "equally yoked" with Christ will provide the foundation we need to make it the right way with others.

I lost everything but yet gained everything at the same time. I have gotten married twice in my life now, even though I had never really thought about marriage. The first time I got married, I thought it was the right thing to do, especially since I was trying to live for Christ. I wanted to go to pre-marital counseling, but my first wife was not in agreement with it, because she was in a hurry to get married. It did not work out because of the issues she brought into the marriage and the undercover issues that I also brought in the marriage.

The thing about "baggage" if it is not dealt with from the beginning or in the past relationship, it will fall into the next relationship and create disharmony.

"Baggage" from previous relationships can come in many forms, including insecurity, low self-esteem, children, false accusations, or anything that is placed "first" before Christ. All these things "can and will" manifest themselves within the marriage. These were some of the things I had to deal with during my first marriage. When I was accused of doing things that I did not do, my pride then stepped in and allowed me to do what I was accused of doing. I messed up by cheating because she said I was cheating.

That is how my relationship was like without God, I was not seeking Him like I use to and applying His word to be a better man. I am selfish by nature and was not really focusing on putting God first, nor my family. I focused on working my job, taking care of my family, then God but not truly giving him the glory that was due him.

The toughest thing I had to go through with my wife was the divorce. Knowing we could have made it work if we had gone to counseling and placed God in the center of our relationship. As I mentioned before, she had lots of baggage from her ex-husband, and she did not express it to me in the beginning. We should have waited at least another six months to a year before marriage, but we started having sex, which messed up the divine chemistry that God wanted in a marriage.

We can use the example in the Bible about Mary, the mother of Jesus. When Joseph first learned that Mary, the person he loved, was pregnant, he was heartbroken but did not want to expose her publicly. We know from reading the story in Matthew 1:18-21, the angel visited him in a dream and told him that Mary was a righteous woman and that she was carrying a child placed in her womb by the Holy Spirit. Certain things must be in place before couples become sexually active. I remember telling my first wife that I did not want to operate this way, but it happened anyway.

I was also still struggling with another relationship that I wanted to get out of with a girl named Rachael. The crazy thing about Rachael is that I had love for her, but I was in love with Emily. That messed me up because I did not take time to get to know Emily how I should have to make an informed decision about our relationship. I did not understand Emily's problems, but I could have been there more for her to understand the pain she was experiencing. I should have been a better listener or giver, but I was more a taker. I was young and dumb, and did not understand what marriage was about, and should have not gotten our families involved in our relationship, which is one of the hardest things we had to learn during this experience.

First, God tells us in Genesis 2:24

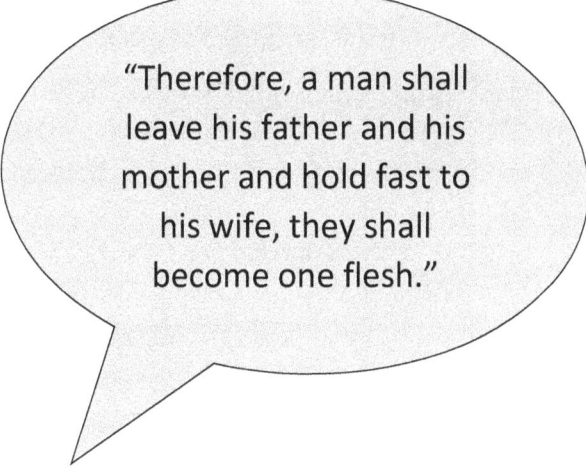

"Therefore, a man shall leave his father and his mother and hold fast to his wife, they shall become one flesh."

But what does "one flesh" mean? It means working as a unit together in doing the true will of God. It also includes being one in sexual activities. One valuable counsel that I would give to anyone in a relationship with a spouse is keeping it between you and the spouse. Do not get family members involved but choose to pray about the situation and seek outside help from a Christian therapist or counselor, if necessary, and not seek the advice of close family or friends because there will be a conflict of interest.

Unfortunately, I learned that the hard way, and it took me about four long years to even think about marrying another person again. Some of the lessons I have learned from my first marriage is spouses should first work on their individual relationship with God and each other as a team. During that time, they will start to become one with each other by actually listening and communicating about one another's flaws, pains or hurt. They can then be open with their relationship to each other, and with God.

> GOD ALREADY KNOWS WHAT EACH OF YOU HAVE GONE THROUGH

Becoming one means that they will share everything as a couple or a unit. I am a firm believer that if individuals are truly honest about their relationship with each other, they would be able to decide if that is the relationship they want or not. Persons must ensure that the relationship they are in has a solid foundation in Christ Jesus and they are baptized by God's biblical word. They will then have the support of the church leadership, their families, and, most importantly, the help of God, our Heavenly Father. When couples joined according to 1 Corinthians 7: 4, each spouse's body becomes their spouse's, giving up the power of their own body.

> *The key to a successful marriage is to glorify God, and for both to be equally yoked*

Personally, my own foundation is one of the most essential elements in my relationship now. I will take my time; I will not be in a hurry. I see who God wants me to walk with and where He wants me to walk and then take it one step at a time. That is why I have been patient right now, so when God blessed me with a wife, I will know the role I should assume, and I will walk it with Him as my Guide and Leader. I can honestly say, "I now understand that the key to a successful marriage is to glorify God and for both of us to be equally yoked in Christ so we can lead, support, and uplift each other as we hold each other accountable".

With our Heavenly Father, we have all power to know we can make a better decision. This is very crucial for leading by example, which means that I will not tell my wife to do something that I am not willing to do first, then I can hold her accountable by my actions because I believe that our actions can speak more volume than our words. The word of God will keep us both accountable, and we can have a successful marriage in God's kingdom by first submitting ourselves to the word of God and to each other, and then we can set an examples for others to walk this journey with Christ.

Most importantly, we would demonstrate true love because love covers a multitude of sins and hurt, and it is one of the secrets to a successful marriage, which is left up to the spouses to make that decision. Jesus is warning men to read and understand His word and not allow them to leave their minds as is confirmed in Proverbs 5:7 when he says, "Hear me now, therefore, O ye children, and depart not from the words of my mouth." Staying with the word is paramount, but should a man be tempted to marry a woman that is not equally yoked? He further instructed them in Proverbs 5:8-9 to "Remove thy way from her and come not nigh the door of her house unless they give their honor unto another and their years unto the cruel." One of the gifts that God gave to human as an incentive to marriage is sexual intimacy, and this can be seen in 1 Corinthians 7:4 which says, "The wife hath not the power of her own body, but the husband; and likewise, also the husband hath not the power of his own body, but the wife." Married couples should understand that they are supposed to have pleasure and fulfillment in their relationship together, especially sexual.

This is the first key, and I am looking forward to what God will do next as I am also extremely excited to talk about part 2, which is Counting the cost in the relationship. It will be a challenge for many relationships because most of them do not count the cost. After all, some do not understand what counting the cost truly entails, and some do not know that they need to count the cost of their relationship.

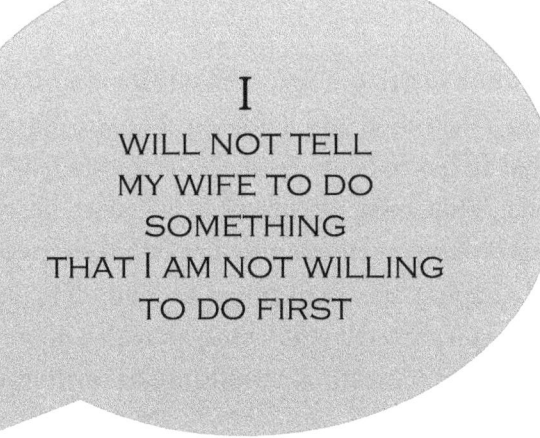

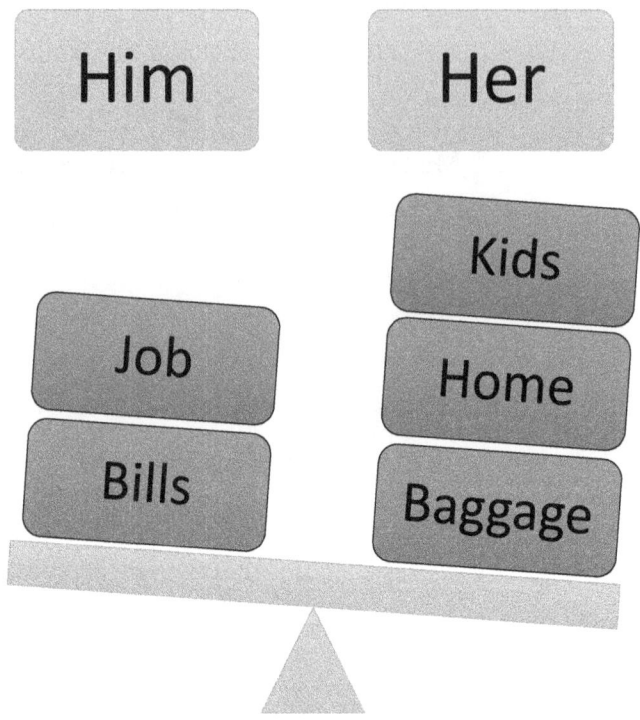

Most marriages are often unbalanced. One has more to do than the other, and neither truly realizing all involved and what all has to be done on a daily basses. Not discussing the home, kids, bills, or if there is baggage. Never drawing the lines or knowing the limits. They think they have it under control. Laying the foundation and building on top, one heavy weight after the other. Only to realize there is no love, patience, communication. friendship, or spiritual guidance.

Part 2
Counting The Cost In The Relationship

The second key to a successful marriage is counting the cost in the relationship. The mistake many people make when getting into a relationship is not taking the time to think about the severity of starting a relationship that will lead to marriage. Marriage is forever until death causes a separation. So, it is choosing a lifetime partner (that you will as a unit) glorify God in every area of life. Luke 14:25-35 gave the analogy that supposing someone wants to build a tower. Would not they first sit down and estimate the cost to see if they have enough money to complete it. If not, they will lay the foundation and not be able to finish it, everyone who sees it would ridicule you saying, "this man began to build and unable to finish."

The scriptures also continue with the metaphor of a king going to war with another king and conclude that he would need to see if he is able to conquer the army with the men that he has and if he is unable to go up against them, he would instead send a delegate with a peace agreement. This the Bible says, is the same way, if we are not willing to give up everything and put Him in control of our lives, we cannot be called His disciples (vs. 33). Counting the cost ensures that each spouse thinks carefully about the consequence of joining as one and recognize that God should be the reason you make any decisions in life, so He should be your number one. A Christ-like relationship is supposed to be forever, so it is a life partner you choose until either one of the persons dies or when God comes.

I did not count the cost in my past relationships because my attraction was more physical, and I did not know what I needed to do or how it was to be done within my two first marriages. During those times in my life, I had no idea what a genuine relationship meant until I got saved and developed a relationship with Christ. I was naïve to the fact that there was more to starting a relationship other than being physical or sexual. In my first marriage, I married an older woman, and I felt it was forced. We did not take the chance to get to know each other honestly; neither did we get pre-marital counseling. If these things were done, I would have known about her previous marriage distresses, and I was not open with her either. Also, in my second marriage, I did not count the cost because I was more captivated by her beauty, youth, and physical appearance. I was also fascinated by her cooking and sexual pleasures.

I was to be blamed because I got caught up with the physical acts and not the spiritual encounter. It is possible if I had only counted the cost in both marriages, I might not have married the first wife because of all the distresses she carried with her. As a young man there was a lot of pressure on me as I did not know how to be a man and take care of her and her two kids because I did not know how to in fact cover her in marriage.

> **Think carefully about the Consequences**

In the second marriage, I probably would not have married her either because I felt my attraction was purely physical and that she used me as a "scapegoat". There was not genuinely godly love on either side. She had a young son that I also care about, and without hesitation, she took her son from me who also loved me as a father. It is essential to learn the background of the individual and all involved of whom you are interested in spending the rest of your life with to determine the type of marriage you will have. I did not know that the people I chose to date in my pass would also reflect within my future relationships. So, getting to know a person and learning their history can give you a lot of information of who that person truly is. It was after these circumstances that I heard God's still voice teaching me about relationships and what it cost.

I did not understand what it means to count the cost in a relationship because I did not realize that everything in life has a cost. As a believer, I must count the cost every day in my relationship with Christ and to walk in His word's regarding my purpose and how to full be a better man and husband.

As a believer, I also must sacrifice the cost for another human being, which means that I must be willing to die for my brothers and sisters. My goal is to bring others closer to Christ and have a fruitful relationship with Him, as our relationships on earth should center around bringing souls to God's Kingdom. When God blesses me with a wife, as Jacob said, "As for me and my house, we will serve the Lord." I am learning that this journey will not be possible without the indwelling of the Holy Spirit to guide us through the thick valleys and plains. We are sinful people by nature and may sin daily against the flesh.

The lust of the flesh, the lust of the eyes, and the pride of life are the things causing us men to fail in our walk with God. As people, we will need to decide whom we will serve and how we will serve Him. In selecting a lifetime partner, we must be able to say individually, "how can I benefit the other, and how can that person benefit me?"

We must be willing to sincerely love unconditionally because that is how God loves us, and since we know we were born in sin and shaped in iniquity, it will take the Divine Spirit to accomplish this task. I am looking forward to getting married one day, and I am looking forward to counting the cost as we discuss if we want kids or not, what our careers will be, and how we can accomplish the will that our Heavenly Father has for us. I am not looking to get married just to be married; I am looking to honor and glorify God through my marriage so that I can have the opportunity to do it God's way so that He alone will get all the praises and the glory that is so rightfully due him.

True Love is Obtainable through the Divine Spirit

By getting married Christ's way, people can and will get saved. I believe I am called to help men to understand what it means to be in a marriage and to stay in marriage the way God intended for us so that He alone will be glorified. Counting the cost as a couple is all about both individuals understanding each other and truly glorifying God together. When we disobey God's word, we are bound to be devastated by the consequences associated with having our own way and ignoring the right direction that the Lord is showing us.

Proverbs highlights some of the reasons persons are to count the cost involved in developing a relationship. For men, Proverb 21:19 says, "it is better to dwell in the wilderness, than with a contentious and an angry woman." Likewise, for women, Proverb 16:32 shows us that it is "Better a patient person than a warrior, one with self-control than one who takes a city." Scriptures have supported the unity of marriages that embrace excellent communication, sexual intimacy, close connections, and firm demonstration of the knowledge of God (Song of Solomon 4:3-7).

> *Jacob said,*
>
> *"As for me and my house, we will serve the Lord."*

Part 3

Deny Yourself, And Pick Up The Cross And Follow Me

3A – Denying yourself

The third key to a Successful Marriage that we will look at is denying yourself and take up the cross. In Matthew 16:24-27, "Then Jesus said to his disciples, "Whoever wants to be my disciple must deny themselves and take up their cross and follow me. For whoever wants to save their life will lose it, but whoever loses their life for me will find it. What good will it be for someone to gain the whole world, yet forfeit their soul? Or what can anyone give in exchange for their soul? For the Son of Man is going to come in his Father's glory with his angels, and then he will reward each person according to what they have done."

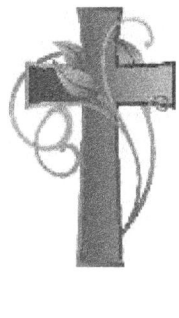

This key will consist of two parts, A and B. Denying yourself will involve putting someone else first. In any solid relationship, individuals must learn how to deny themselves as they walk out this road of life, because by nature, we are selfish beings, especially men. Women however naturally demonstrate a nurturing and supportive attitude, even though some women may not exhibit those traits. God made man and women in unique ways, which can be seen in Ephesians 5:25 when the Holy Bible said, "Husbands, love your wives, just as Christ also loved the church and gave Himself for her" and 1 Peter 3:1 declares, "wives should respect and submit to their own husbands."

> *She is not as strong as a man*

In the Bible, the book of 1 Peter 3 entails lessons for both husbands and wives in how they are to treat each other and their physical appearance. The Bible also says in verse 7 that "Husbands, also live with your wife the way you know is right. Respect her because she is a woman. She is not as strong as a man. Also, respect her because God has given her and you the blessings of life. In this way, you will not stop God from doing what you ask him to do." This verse confirms that when man disobeys God and does not honor his wife, it can prevent his prayers from being answered. Verse 8 likewise says, "finally, all of you, be like-minded, be sympathetic, love one another, be compassionate and humble." As couples, we must exhibit these qualities within our marriage, and these characteristics will draw others to God. As men of Christ, we are to lead by example, which means that we must first deny ourselves.

Adam and Eve experienced the same issue in the Garden of Eden. The serpent made Eve questioned God and saw that the apple looked pleasant to the eye and the one that was good to gain knowledge. This illustrates the lust of the eye, the lust of the flesh, and the pride of life. She did not understand that God already planted everything in her that she needed, maybe she thought she needed something more apart from God. Many people in relationships today think they need more than what God has already placed in them.

When we deny ourselves, it is a sacrifice that will make a person uncomfortable. Denying yourselves means that you are putting your hope in someone else and trusting that person to lead you in the right direction. So, when a man denies himself and takes up his cross to follow Jesus Christ, he tells God to take control of his life and be ruler and Head of his life, and by extension, his household. It is important to note that we can deny ourselves but still not truly follow God and where he is actually leading us, and in this case, the marriage cannot work. It can work only when both partners follow and place God, the Savior, at the forefront of their minds and obey His leadership.

This is why key number three (3) consists of two parts, first denying self and taking up the cross. A husband that is willing to obey God's direction will be more apt to die for his family, faith, and everything God placed before him. When you deny yourself, you will take responsibility when things go wrong because you will be more willing to say, "Yes, baby, it is my fault and I take responsibility as a man because I should have been careful, or I should have been more alert." The cross will be more comfortable to carry when we deny ourselves because they go together. Our life is but a vapor that will vanish, so too is how time goes by in life. Most people do not follow God from the beginning because they believe His foundation is out of order and does not align with their beliefs. This practice will take time for some, but only with prayer and supplication with thanksgiving will God make it possible, according to Philippians 4:6. Denying yourself is possible through the grace of our Lord and Savior, Jesus Christ.

> Denying yourself is possible through the grace of our Lord and Savior, Jesus Christ

Also, through Christ, the barriers between persons have been removed because to be near to Him is to be near to others. For example, a genuine union to be demonstrated in the family circle, it requires compatibility with Christ as stated in Galatians 5:24 – 25 which reads, "And they that are Christ's have crucified the flesh with the affections and lusts. (25) "If we live in the Spirit, let us also walk in the Spirit." (26) "Let us not be desirous of vain glory, provoking one another, envying one another." Denying yourself involved refusing to take up the world's desires in its sinful form and join with the Holy Spirit for directions in all areas of your lives.

Part 3B – Pick Up Your Cross and Follow Me

Part B of key number three is taking up the cross after you have denied yourself. In discussing denying yourself means to evaluate yourself and make sacrifices because we, as men, have a complex of being in charge, being the boss and being the head of the household that we miss the real purpose for our existence. Without first understanding our role as men, according to God's word, most men do not realize that we must deny ourselves to lead by example and give to God first. As a leader in God's household, we must show example for our wives, our children, and also our community because denying ourselves take sacrifice. When couples become one, it is crucial that men carry the cross because this pleases God. How two can become one flesh is when you die to the flesh and take up your cross. Unfortunately, most persons are not aware that the race of life sometimes can be like a marathon  because it takes time and practice to master, and that time and training have to be performed based on requirements outlined by God in His word. One of the biggest things for most women is that they like to see examples.

They want to follow a man of God and desire to have a relationship with God just as they desire to have a relationship with a man, but we must be willing to let them know that we would die for them just as Christ died for the church. In deciding which woman, you want to be with, you must look at yourself and evaluate yourself. Self-reflection and self-awareness are essential in any real relationship and especially when it involves a spouse. Self-reflection allows us to examine our true actions, emotions, and the things that we genuinely feel. Philippians 4:8 says "Finally, brethren, whatsoever things are true, whatsoever things are honest, whatsoever things are just, whatsoever things are pure, whatsoever things are lovely, whatsoever things are of good report; if there be any virtue, and if there be any praise, think on these things.

A vital question to ask ourselves as husbands is, "are we willing to die for our wives like Christ died for us and carry our cross?" Which symbolizes that Christ also picked up the cross all the way to Calvary. Christ did not have to carry His cross, but He did as an example for us. In the Books of the Gospel, Jesus always alluded to the importance of taking the cross and following Him. He is saying to men that they are to sacrifice for that woman; be willing to die for her, be an example for her to follow and hear her when she speaks. When we lead by God's standard and walk in the footsteps of Christ, it would be easier for us to sacrifice for the women. As God is the head of Christ, Christ is the head of the man, and man is the head of the woman, so we must  lead by example. How can individuals actually say that they are a true disciple of Christ, true sons and daughters, and ambassadors of Christ if they have never picked up the cross? The "one you feed is the one that will lead," and the one that you let lead you is the one that will revere you.

As a man thinketh, so is he. This is confirmed in Matthew 15:18, which says, "but those things which proceed out of the mouth come from the heart, and they defile a man."

I did not know these scriptures before I got married, and that is the reason they did not work because I was not applying biblical principles to my marriage and spirituals keys in my relationship with Christ. I was ignorant of this type of revelation and caught up in my selfish ways.

Since then, I have realized that I must pick up my cross and follow Christ, and now I have become a better man because I lead by first submitting myself to God. I want to lead by giving, so I must be willing to give. I cannot be a taker in this relationship; I must be a giver in the relationship first, so my wife will be able to give more and meet in the middle. In most things, I should lead out first, such as in my attitude, prayer life, reading the Word of God, and leading her to church because she is my helpmate. She is not my slave, servant, but support and companion for me. The Message Bible says it this way in 1 Peter 3:7 that "the same goes for the husbands: Be good husbands to your wives. Honor them, delight in them. As women, they lack some of your advantages. But in the new life of God's grace, you are equals. Treat your wives, then, as equals so your prayers do not run aground." God has called her to respect me, not to love me, but He has called me to love her and called her to respect me, so I must be willing to die for her.

If we choose to lead by example, our wives should not have any reason for disobeying or disrespecting us. If this should happen, then we need to deny ourselves, by doing things God's ways, pick up the cross, by still showing respect and leaving the situation in His Hands. 1 Peter 5:7 says, "casting all your care upon him; for He cares for you." Women are to be mindful that while some men may not be at the same levels as they are, the Bible supports them submitting and treating their husbands with respect. The Holy Word said that when the unbelieving men see the love and nurture in their wives' behavior, they can turn to God as stated in (1 Peter 3:1).

This situation will identify those who are living by God's commandments and those who have not become new creatures by allowing old habits to be in the past and pick up new ones through Christ Jesus, as stated in 2 Corinthians 5:17. If we prayerfully leave things in God's Hands, He has promised to take care of our heavyweight according to Isaiah 41:10 which declares, "Fear not, for I am with you; be not dismayed, for I am your God; I will strengthen you, I will help you, I will uphold you with my righteous right hand." By doing this, I will be in line with my responsibility, and I can become the true leader he has called me to be.

The thing is we are not perfect, but we serve a perfect God. So, by in fact serving a perfect God, He will give us the wisdom, knowledge and understand to know how to walk this journey. The "one we feed is the one that will lead" and we will eventually become slaves to which will only lead to destruction. I have chosen to feed my spirit so that I can be spiritually fulfilled and not my flesh because it is a mess.

As a man of God, this is the third key to a successful marriage in God's Kingdom. Deny yourself and take up your cross (as we walk this out) we know it will be challenging, but we can overcome all things through the supernatural power of the Holy Spirit. Another important fact that men are to be mindful of in their relationships is truly how to treat their wives. Colossians 3:19 states, "Husbands, love your wives and do not be harsh with them" (NIV). This is not an acceptable behavior in the Kingdom of God. When both partners feel loved and respected in their relationship, with God as number one and their anchor; disagreements will be handled in a much healthier way. Women must be treated as the virtuous woman they are (Proverbs 31: 10 – 31) and be loved based on 1 John 4: 11 – 12, which says, "Beloved, if God so loved us, we ought also to love one another." (12) "No man hath seen God at any time. If we love one another, God dwelleth in us, and His love is perfected in us."

Part 4
Renewing Your Mind

This is essentially one of the most crucial of all the keys discussed - Renewing our minds. Unfortunately, many people are not aware that renewing their mind calls for them to be intentional in allowing their mind to be renewed God's way, for instance in their relationships with others, with their spouse, their spiritual walk with God, and their lifestyle. Romans 12:1- 2 states, be transformed by the renewing of our mind. This is the same principle that must be applied in our marriages. People need to know that we must renew our minds daily because there will be good days and bad ones. There will also be days that we are up and some when we are down, happy, and sad days too, like an emotional roller coaster ride.

Women's minds are more like a battlefield with their emotions, which will play an essential part in your walk and relationship in your marriage. This is when men must lead by example by renewing their minds and showing their wives what it means to renew their minds.

It is crucial to pray as a couple and ask God to teach us how to renew our minds in this relationship so we can be more robust for Him and each other. This is the most crucial part of any relationship if you want to be successful in your relationship for God's kingdom. Communicate with her and say, "Honey, let us pray about renewing our minds." You will run across many bumps in the road because the enemy will come to you on either side. For me, the enemy has now been evicted because I understand what he is always trying to do to affect  me, and now I know what it means to be in a real relationship with someone. I will be patient in getting married the next time, and that means putting everything before God in prayer first, then waiting and listening to hear His reply.

By doing this, my wife, as my helpmate, will actually understand how crucial our journey will be, and this action will even prevent us from fighting over every minor thing that arises in our relationship. Yet, if issues do show up, we will handle it more easily with God's Spirit. We can also agree to disagree on things but still agree on God's way. I am not expecting my wife to be perfect, because neither am I, and it would be unfair for an imperfect person like myself to seek out an ideal woman; and expect her to be perfect.

Nevertheless, I will always be looking for her to use wisdom in our relationship and be wise as a serpent but yet gentle as a dove. I will likewise show her that I too will be an example for her to follow because I will seek counsel, advice, and God in prayer to speak to me through His Word for our marriage to succeed. The person I will marry would be my best friend, my lover, and my wife. I want to be able to talk to her about anything and everything. I will be open and totally transparent for her with nothing to hide. Being open, respectful, honest, and willing to listen to each other's opinions is vital in a marriage. Unfortunately, a lot of times, people get married for the wrong reasons and not realizing that marriage takes work.

I firmly believe that if we in fact get counsel before marriage and lay all the "cards" on the table, we will not need to be worried about the finances or other things presented because scriptures told us that we are to seek God first and all things would be added to us. He knows what we want before we ask, so He would provide all we need to live the life He calls us to live. Our responsibility would be whether we are equally yoked, whether we count the full cost in the relationship, deny ourselves, or actually pick up the cross and renew our minds daily as a children of God.

These four keys are foundational in any relationship, and if these are present in our marriage, I know my wife and I will have success in our union. As it pertains to our finances, we can make money and have a lovely house because God promises to make a way out for us. We can also raise our kids as disciples of God because we are in the right church, the right house, and getting the right word. That is why we need to recognize that renewing the mind takes work, time, and preparation. As men, we need to understand that as we walk out this life, we need to be the example by first showing our wives how to do the same by how much we spend time with God in prayers and through His Word. This would prove how essential He is in our lives and also in our marriages.

As a married couple, I would want my wife and I to seek the same thing based on Biblical principles commanded in scriptures. These also include putting God first, then our families, then others, and living the example God instructed us by loving neighbors and spreading the good news of Jesus Christ. This means that even when there are disagreements, still being respectful with each other should be the main contributing factor in everything we do as a couple. A lot of people want God's principles to work, but people are not saved. The world is crazy because the same percentage of divorce in the world is in the church. So, you ask yourself the question, what are we doing wrong in the church? Surly we must be doing something wrong for such a high rate of divorce to be in the body of Christ. If we were doing it right by God's way, there would be no divorce, or the percentage would be extremely low.

So, I am here to tell you that renewing your mind is ultimately the most crucial part of any relationship. If you cannot renew your mind, there will be disharmony and a red flag somewhere. Being emotional creatures, women will, from time to time, go through something emotional, so it is crucial that we, as men, will be there for them, protect them, respect, honor, and cover them in every way because we need to cultivate and support our wives. This means that we must help them through their issues and find ways to resolve them when their past and present hurt present themselves.

Protect	Respect
Honor	Cover
Cultivate	Support

However, this can only truly be possible when they are open and honest with us. We should develop a game plan on capturing her heart and encouraging her the right way. We also need to know how to uplift her when she is down, purposefully listens to her when she speaks, and love her in such a way that she will see the character of God in me that will make her proud to be called my wife.

The truth behind walking with Christ in life is not all about us, but it is to glorify God in our relationship and to help the other person to walk it out and keep them secure. Marriage is about glorifying God and cultivating the woman the way the Lord intended in His commandments.

By the way, you support her will lift her self-esteem, and she will feel that she is a blessing to you and will, in turn, bless you with the qualities she also possesses. I would not expect my wife to do anything for me that I would not do for her. I should not expect my wife to "jump over a mountain" if I am not willing to do the same for her first. We need to realize that renewing the mind daily is essential to the four keys, and as we as men renew our minds, we also empower women to renew theirs for the Kingdom of God. When we look around, we see there are more women in church than men. Why is that so? Because men are selfish by nature, and we do not fear God enough to give Him our time? Or is it because men are not humble enough to put all his care into another Person's Hands? Whatever the reason is, God is waiting for men to step up and be the person He intends them to be for His Kingdom. On the other hand, the women will run to God; they would go to church, get involved, and bring the kids with them while the men stay home. Men, you are called to renew your mind to give God all the glory and time that is due to Him and Him alone.

2 Corinthians 10:5 says,

> "Casting down imaginations, and every high thing that exalted itself against the knowledge of God and bringing into captivity every thought to the obedience of Christ."

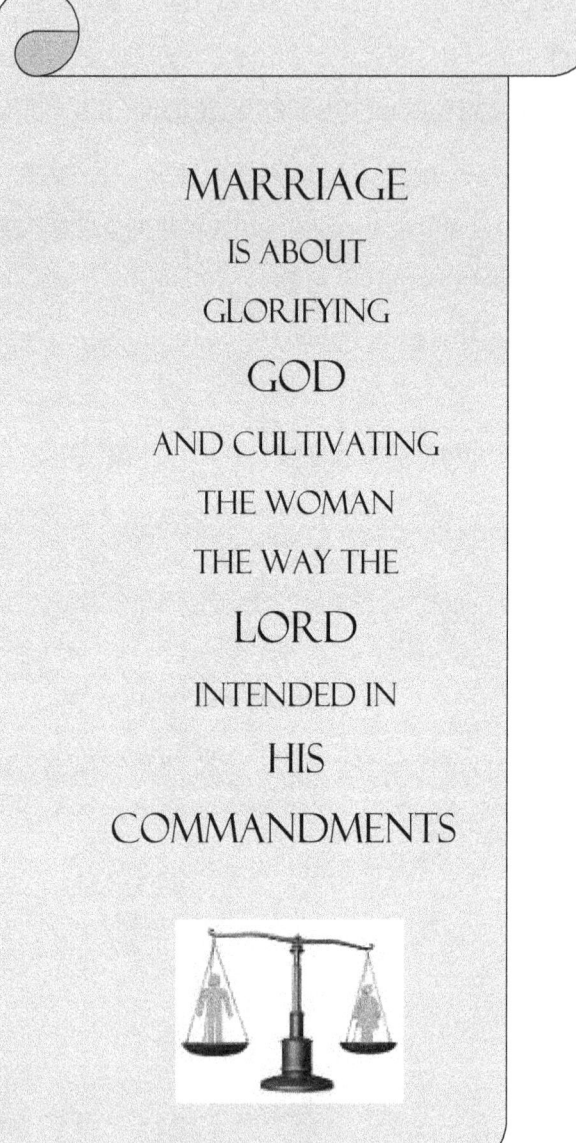

CONCLUSION

Before we step out in Christ, our first business as Christians is to pray, and praying is having a conversation with God. Genesis 2:24 also reveals that God charged men that they should leave their parents and join with their wives, where they will become one flesh. The way God designed marital happiness for the family structure can be seen in Ephesian 5: 21-25, in which He calls for wives to respect their husbands, and the husbands being the head of the wives are to love them, just as Christ loves the church and gave His life for it. This builds a Christian household.

For a couple to be effective in creating a home of reverence for God, an equally supportive attitude must be demonstrated by both the husband and the wife. Also, in Ephesian 6, 1-4 children are also commanded to obey their parents in the Lord, for this is right, and to honor their father and their mother which is the first commandment with a promise. He further instructs fathers not to provoke their children, causing them to be in a rage, but instead to grow them up in love and the knowledge of God.

To display the importance of marriage in God's eyes, He equated it to the model of Christ's love for the church in which each member of the family has a responsibility and should perform their role in ensuring that the whole family is secured. When we examined the book of Proverbs, we can clearly see how it concentrates on the relationships in the family through instructions and encouragement.

This is important because you get into marriage to glorify God and not just each other. By doing that, you could also bring others closer to God when they see your marriage blossoming and ask, what is the secret to your satisfying relationship. You show me someone who counts God in their relationship, and I will show you one that is still married today. Also, if you show me an equally yoked person, I will show you someone who is still married—being compatible means that you and your partner agree to disagree, which allows you to get along with each other when things are good and when they are not so good. I Corinthians 1:10 says that we are to be perfectly united in mind and thought.

I am a recovering drug addict and alcoholic, so this journey for me is the real thing. I used to visit the porn sites regularly, but by the Holy Spirit, I am no longer doing those things that are not a good representation of God's Kingdom. We ought to ask for repentance today, so tomorrow, we can be a better child of the Living God. I will need to die to self before, so I can be whom I am destined to be in the Savior's eyes.

When a couple steps out into their communities, despite the actual reason for their trip or activities, they are representing Jesus Christ. They do not need to scream, wear a sign or say that they are Christians to everybody they meet, but their characteristics should already display their level of commitment to the Heavenly Savior. It is the same way in developing a marriage; once the right features and attributes are evident in each spouse, persons who see them can know that their friendship is already based on God's principles. I Corinthians 10:31 clearly stated that whatever we do, in private or public, should all be done for God's glory. At the end of our life, we hope to hear these words from the One above, "Well done, good and faithful servant!" (Matthew 25:23). Spiritually, we need each other to walk with God first, then with family, friends, and those we will encounter in our lives.

We will not pretend that loneliness does not exist, and we must know that it can be a challenge when emotions arise, such as feeling unloved and unappreciated. However, when we take time out to seek God first, not just for any male or female to come into our lives, but for us to meet the right companion who will truly love and respect you the way God intended it to happen. Usually, during our relationships as young adults, we tend to focus mostly on physicality versus spirituality. During those times, we usually behave like we are in total control of our lives without a Spiritual being to guide us. Then when we got to a stage and realized that we are getting older and not finding the right woman for us, we start blaming every woman but ourselves.

Nevertheless, according to the Holy Word, we keep failing because God was not in the forefront of our minds; carnality was what we eat, slept, and song. Once we start putting the Father in the center of our lives, we would start seeing successes in our endeavors and would not have to look far or hard to know the person God wants us to date, then married. We also need to understand that by getting sexually active with an individual before seeking Christ's direction and getting the approval to go to the next step, is when we give the devil a foothold in our lives as stated in (Ephesians 4:27). Submit yourselves first to God, resist the devil, and he will flee from you says, (James 4:7). Our bodies are God's temple, as stated in (1 Corinthians 3:16-17), which speaks, "don't you know that you yourselves are God's temple and that God's Spirit dwells in your midst? If anyone destroys God's temple, God will destroy that person; for God's temple is sacred, and you together are that temple."

We are blessed to know that in the Holy Bible, we have all the instructions and directions we can ever need in any situation. 2 Timothy 3:16-17 says,

> "All Scripture is God-breathed and is useful for teaching, rebuking, correcting, and training in righteousness so that the servant of God may be thoroughly equipped for every good work.

Our Heavenly Father loves us so much that He ensures that we are prepared and have all the tools needed before stepping out. We have that responsibility to ensure that we use all the resources He provided so we can be the best husbands and spouses for our partner. We all need human connection because God created us that way so He wants us to find the right person so our lives can reflect Him.

Do two walk together unless they have agreed to do so? (Amos 3:3). We know that a house that is divided against itself cannot stand, so as a man, do not bring division in your home, and the only way you know how to do that is when you have a stable relationship with Christ. I am willing to drive in the back seat or the trunk just to make God the Driver of my life. I have Peter's tendencies and Paul's conviction; I know where I was, and I know where I am going now.

The First Key

A Marriage is In Fact to Glorify God

The Second Key

Is Counting the Spiritual Cost of the Relationship

The Third Key

Looks at Denying Yourself and Picking Up the Cross

The Fourth Key

Is to

Renew the

Mind

by

Being Still

Get Your Copy at
AMAZON.COM

Equally Yoked; The Four Keys to a Successful Marriage in God's Kingdom

www.ingramcontent.com/pod-product-compliance
Lightning Source LLC
Chambersburg PA
CBHW031212090426
42736CB00009B/886